corepilates

discover your **longest,**
leanest body with pilates on the ball

Published by ABC Books for the
AUSTRALIAN BROADCASTING CORPORATION
GPO Box 9994 Sydney NSW 2001

First published September 2003
Reprinted September 2003

National Library of Australia
Cataloguing-in-publication entry
King, Michael.
  Corepilates : discover you longest, leanest body with pilates on the ball.
  ISBN 0 7333 1240 3.
  1. Pilates method. 2. Stretching exercises. 3. Muscle
  strength. 4. Physical fitness. I. Australian Broadcasting
  Corporation. II.
  Title.
613.71

Designed by Ingo Voss, voss design
Photographs of Olivia Bell by Hugh Hamilton
Photography by Jon Reid
Clothes by Bloch, Brazil Body

Colour reproduction by Colorwize, Adelaide
Printed and bound in Hong Kong by Quality Printing

5 4 3 2

AV

MICHAEL KING

Michael has been educating people in many facets of the fitness industry since 1979. He trained with the London School of Contemporary Dance, and then combined his dance training with his fitness career as a Pilates trainer and adult exercise instructor at the Pineapple Dance Studio in London. Since then he has worked with dance companies and fitness organisations all over the world, notably with the Houston Ballet, where he worked on such prestigious productions as *Swan Lake, The Sleeping Beauty* and *Daphnis and Chloe*. In Los Angeles he taught for five years at the Voight Fitness and Dance Studio, where he had an extensive celebrity client list.

Now based in London, Michael splits his time between choreography, presentations at international conventions and direction of a variety of fitness programs. He works from his studio and training centre, the Pilates Institute in London, and, with the Pilates Institute team, is the training provider for Pilates in many of the national fitness chains in the United Kingdom and around the world.

Michael has always used Pilates as the backbone of his teaching, as its principles apply to every type of physical activity. In his own words, 'My greatest joy is to see this new movement in the fitness industry for this technique. I hope to pass on the information I have learned to you, and that you will benefit from this great work, as I have.'

TABLE OF CONTENTS

Warming up

On the mat

Building strength

Putting it all together

Stretching

THE PILATES PROGRAM

Pilates (pronounced pi/**lah**/tees) is an exercise program designed to make your body stronger and more structurally efficient. 'Structurally' is the keyword: Pilates focuses on strengthening your body's core muscles — the muscles that surround and support your trunk — so that you will feel fitter, stand taller, and be better able to cope with life in today's demanding world.

Many exercise programs concentrate on developing outer muscle strength through weight training, exercise bikes, treadmills and so on.

Pilates, by contrast, aims to develop the whole body, giving you a longer, leaner, stronger look. It is based on exercises that you can do at home, with only a small outlay on equipment and no expensive gym subscriptions. You can even practise some Pilates techniques while you are driving, working, standing in the supermarket checkout queue, or watching television.

Modern life makes unprecedented demands on our bodies. A hundred years ago we would have been bending and stretching in the fields or in a factory, or standing at a tall Victorian writing desk, or cleaning the house without the aid of labour-saving devices. But today most of us spend many hours bent over a waist-high desk or sitting at a computer, with our bodies leaning forward to read or write. We are training our bodies into a rounded posture that cramps the muscles around the front of our ribs, strains our back muscles, weakens our pelvic floor muscles and inhibits our breathing.

It is a lifestyle that can be damaging, both physically and emotionally. The Pilates method can teach you to counteract the damage by retraining your body to work better, stretching tight muscles and strengthening weak ones, and improving overall physical fitness and mental wellbeing.

Working with the ball

COREPILATES combines the Pilates method with the exercise ball — a strong, inflatable plastic ball that introduces a challenging element of instability into any exercise you perform on it to improve your body balance and strengthen your spine.

Not so much a program, more a way of life

Pilates confers benefits way beyond improved strength and wellbeing. It is:

> **TIME-EFFICIENT** – you can do it almost anywhere, anytime

> **COST-EFFICIENT** – little expensive equipment, no gym subscriptions

> **ADAPTABLE** – suitable for everybody, from dancers to people with disabilities or injuries

PILATES THEN AND NOW

JOSEPH Hubertus Pilates was born in Düsseldorf in 1880 and died in New York City in 1967. As a child he was plagued with asthma, rickets and rheumatic fever, so his parents enrolled him in a gymnastics school to build up his strength. Against all the odds he became an outstanding gymnast, and when he left school he joined a circus and began to teach boxing.

When World War I broke out, Pilates was in England giving boxing classes at Scotland Yard. As a German national he was interned in a camp, where he introduced an exercise program that is believed to have saved many of the inmates during the influenza epidemic of 1918–19, which is estimated to have killed as many as 40 million people worldwide.

Transferred to a hospital, he applied the same exercise principles to the patients, again with outstanding success in promoting recuperation and rehabilitation.

After the war Pilates returned briefly to Germany, disliked what he saw, and emigrated to America, where he opened an exercise studio. Eventually he published a manual describing 34 exercises, which has become a reference point for Pilates teachers all over the world.

Pilates today

But Pilates' original exercise program presupposes a body at the peak of physical condition, and is not suitable for a fitness novice: nothing is more discouraging than being asked to do the impossible.

So contomporary Pilates instructors apply Pilates' original principles, but with modifications designed to build up functional fitness at a pace adapted to individual needs. A modern Pilates program may include as many as 500 exercises.

You will feel the benefits of Pilates almost immediately, but it is not a quick fix. It is a long-term investment that will give you core strength and a supple, lean physique. By working your mind and your body together it will promote physical and mental awareness and encourage a calm focus in everything you do.

Pilates and the dancers

Pilates' work in America brought him into contact with dancers, notably Martha Graham, herself a revolutionary in the science of movement. She sent her dancers to Pilates' studio, and the program quickly became known as a dancers' technique.

Pilates and Graham were both strong personalities and eventually they clashed, but over the years many dancers have used Pilates techniques to strengthen their bodies and to recover from injuries. Unlike exercise programs that bulk up the muscles, Pilates develops the long muscles and controlled, graceful movements that dancers aim for.

EIGHT PRINCIPLES OF PILATES

1 Concentration

Many exercise programs let you 'switch off', but Pilates links every movement to a thought process. It is a thinking way of moving, a mind–body technique that requires total focus on your body. You must block out extraneous thoughts and concentrate on your movements.

2 Breathing

Correct breathing is essential to Pilates, yet it can be the most difficult part of the program to master. The better your breath control, the more effective Pilates will be for you. Your breathing must drive your movements, not the other way around.

3 Centering

If you have a sedentary lifestyle, the right kind of exercise will develop deep muscle strength to help you sit correctly and avoid lower back problems. When you practise Pilates, you focus on the centre of your body, its powerhouse. You are developing core strength.

4 Control

Slow and controlled movement is the key to Pilates, with each phase moving slowly and smoothly into the next. This develops both physical and mental control; you will become aware of your body as never before.

5 Precision

For dancers, precision is not just desirable but essential for their physical safety: each movement, and the whole sequence of movements, must be perfectly coordinated, otherwise they risk failure and injury. We cannot all be dancers, but Pilates can teach us to move so as to avoid fatigue and pain.

6 Movement

Pilates is a continuous cycle of related movements, each flowing smoothly and unhurriedly into the next. Pilates can be combined with other forms of exercise to ensure that you are using your full range of movement.

7 Isolation

In Pilates, 'isolation' is the mental exercise of identifying the feel of all your muscle groups. Only then can you work to strengthen weaker muscles and bring your whole muscular structure into harmony.

8 Routine

Set aside some time each day for your Pilates exercises, just as you do to shower, dress and prepare for work. Give your muscles the same regular attention as you give your skin and hair, and your body will reward you with a better performance, both mentally and physically.

FOR many people, correct breathing is the most difficult part of Pilates to learn. This is because it does not feel like a natural way of breathing.

Most of us have two ways of breathing. When we are at rest we breathe shallowly, using only the upper part of the chest. When we are working hard physically we breathe more deeply, using our abdominal muscles, in order to take in more oxygen.

For Pilates, however, we need to use a breathing technique called lateral thoracic breathing. This is because Pilates requires a partial contraction of the core muscles of the lower abdomen, so that we cannot use those muscles to take in the air we need for physical exertion.

Basic breathing drill

To practise lateral thoracic breathing, place your hands horizontally around the base of your ribcage, with your middle fingers just touching each other. Breathe in slowly and deeply, expanding your ribcage at the sides and back, and keeping your shoulders relaxed and low. Your middle fingers should part as your back and lower ribcage expand, and rejoin when you breathe out.

Lateral thoracic breathing

Breathing is controlled by the diaphragm, a large muscle at the base of the ribcage that moves up and down to empty and then fill the lungs. In lateral thoracic breathing we fill the lungs to capacity by using the diaphragm and the muscles of the thorax — the lower chest — to expand the ribcage to its fullest extent.

LOCATING THE CORE

YOUR torso consists of a framework of bones that support and protect your vital organs, and several layers of muscles that give you the strength to stand, to walk and run, to bend and stretch and to carry out the activities of daily life.

The muscles of the outer layer are often referred to as the global muscles. The main one is the rectus abdominis (the 'six-pack'), which runs down the front of the body. Then come the external oblique muscles, and next the internal oblique muscles. In the innermost layer are what we call the local muscles or the core muscles. The great benefit of Pilates is that it not only tones your global muscles and gives you a tight abdomen, it also strengthens the difficult-to-reach core muscles.

The transversus abdominis is the deepest abdominal muscle and the closest to the spine. It is attached to the spine and wraps around the front of the body like an old-fashioned corset. The other important part of the inner muscle layer is the lumbar multifidus, a muscle that runs along the back of the spine in a hairweave pattern. Weakness in the lower parts of this muscle — the lumbar area — is often the cause of the persistent lower back pain that plagues so many people.

Running horizontally above and below these layers of muscle are the diaphragm and the pelvic floor muscles. The diaphragm is a large muscle that sits at the base of your ribcage and powers your breathing. The pelvic floor muscles run from the pubic bone to the coccyx and act as a sling that contains and supports the internal organs of the abdomen.

A helpful way to think of your torso is to imagine that it is a concertina. When the concertina is silent, it is an upright column with strong but flexible sides and firm end-pieces. When it is being played, the column bends and stretches as the player moves the end-pieces to produce sounds by pushing air out or drawing it in.

Think of the muscles of the abdomen and lower back as the sides of the concertina, and your diaphragm and pelvic floor muscles as the end-pieces. When you are sitting at your desk or at the wheel of your car, or waiting in the supermarket checkout queue, these muscles are doing their basic job of keeping your body upright and supplied with oxygen. When you stretch to reach a high shelf or bend to pick up a child, you are 'playing' your 'concertina': your transversus abdominis and lumbar multifidus are working to stretch or bend your body, supported by your pelvic floor muscles and powered by the oxygen you take in using your diaphragm.

Feeling good with Pilates

Pilates training will give you a strong, dynamic spine and a pain-free back, so that you will sit and stand correctly and reach and lift without risking muscle strain or injury. And as a bonus you will have more flexibility and toned muscles. You will find yourself moving freely and gracefully.

STRENGTHENING THE CORE

Developing and enhancing core strength and functional fitness through Pilates centres on these crucial muscles of the lower torso, the transversus abdominis, the lumbar multifidus, the diaphragm, and the pelvic floor. These muscles work in synergy and you need to strengthen all of them to develop functional fitness, improve your posture and maintain a strong spine.

There are plenty of Pilates exercises that are designed to work on the global muscles of the abdomen and will give you tone and definition in this area.

But strengthening only the global muscles is not sufficient to achieve functional fitness. For that you must also train the core muscles. They are made up of different fibres to the global muscles, and they require a different strengthening technique.

Current research suggests that the core muscles are best trained at a contraction of 30 per cent. This sounds impossibly technical, and a precise 30 per cent contraction is measurable only with expensive equipment. But there are visualising techniques that can help you to locate your core muscles so that you will know when you have achieved approximately the right degree of contraction.

ACTIVATING THE CORE

FOR the Pilates beginner, the first step is to locate the key core muscles and to learn how to switch them on to the ideal 30 per cent. Current Pilates practice is to work separately on either the transversus abdominis or the pelvic floor muscles. As they both function together, by activating one group you will activate the other.

It is possible to have impressively well-developed abdominal muscles and still not have efficient core strength. That is because the transversus abdominis is located at a much deeper level than the rectus abdominis and the obliques and is not trained by conventional ab exercises such as crunches. When you first start to focus on this muscle you will not feel any dramatic sensation, but as you improve its tone and endurance you will notice that you can sit and stand comfortably without conscious effort.

If you do have strong abdominal muscles, it may better to focus on contracting the pelvic floor to avoid recruiting them instead of the transversus abdominis.

A weak pelvic floor can destabilise all the muscular structures of the lower back. If you have back pain, you might not associate it with a weak pelvic floor but this is a common source of discomfort, particularly among women. Fortunately it is possible to rebuild strength in this area.

As you progress with your Pilates you may find that in some movements you contract both the transversus abdominis and the pelvic floor to improve your form. Recent research by Australian physiotherapists has demonstrated that doing so results in the messaging between the two muscle groups being broken. It is better to focus exclusively on one group.

We ask a great deal of our bodies, especially those of us who pass the working day behind a desk. Professional sitters spend hours in a forward flexed position and many of us gradually assume a rounded, slumped posture. This results in a weak spine, tightness in the upper back and hamstrings and a spreading abdomen. We can use Pilates to rebalance the body, build strength and correct poor alignment.

How long will this take? The good news is you will see improvements immediately, because as soon as you activate your centre you will look longer and leaner. It will, of course, take time and effort to retrain your muscles to make postural improvements permanent, and will require a partnership between you and your body. Making a

commitment to this partnership will reap huge dividends and it doesn't just come into effect when you are doing a Pilates session. There are plenty of opportunities, even when you are not exercising, to focus on your alignment and activate your centre to strengthen those deep postural muscles.

Activate your centre

An active centre engages your deep muscles and stabilises your spine. When you do the exercises in this book you are instructed repeatedly to 'activate your centre'. This means contracting either the transversus or the pelvic floor to 30 per cent.

Locating the transversus abdominis

Sit upright and imagine that you are wearing a belt with ten notches.

1 Pull your navel towards your spine as far as you can —
the equivalent of the tenth notch on your imaginary belt.
[100 per cent contraction]

2 Release the belt and relax, without letting your spine shorten.
[0 per cent contraction]

3 Tighten the belt to the fifth notch.
[50 per cent contraction]

4 Release the belt and relax.
[0 per cent contraction]

5 Tighten the belt to the third notch.
[30 per cent contraction]

At step 5, you have achieved the ideal transversus abdominis contraction for Pilates work.
Think of holding the contraction softly. If you grip too tightly the muscle will fatigue and
release. You will build better endurance for functional fitness at a contraction of 30 per cent.

Locating the pelvic floor muscles

Imagine that you must control a powerful urge to empty your bladder.
The muscles that you use are the pelvic floor muscles.
Think of these muscles as the lift in a ten-storey building.

1   Tighten the muscles to raise the lift to the tenth floor.
    [100 per cent contraction]

2   Lower the lift to the ground floor.
    [0 per cent contraction]

3   Raise the lift to the fifth floor.
    [50 per cent contraction]

4   Lower the lift to the ground floor.
    [0 per cent contraction]

5   Raise the lift to the third floor.
    [30 per cent contraction]

At step 5, you have achieved the ideal pelvic floor contraction for Pilates work. Try not to activate your glutes (the muscles in your buttocks) when you pull up. You are aiming to recruit the sling of muscle between your pubic bone and your lower back. Some yoga practitioners advocate pulling up through the anus, but the movement in Pilates is more of a lift through the centre.

STANDING TALL

THE English word posture comes from the Italian *postura*, a contraction of the Latin *positura*, which is derived from the verb *ponere*, meaning 'to place'. In its primary sense it expresses the relationship between the body's core structure (the skeleton and the core muscles) and its superficial structure (the outer muscles).

Posture is made up of the body positions that we adopt in response to the various physical and emotional demands that our lives make. Good posture is the body position that the musculoskeletal system needs in order to function with maximum efficiency.

In the best of all possible worlds all the parts of your body would be in exact alignment, allowing you to sit, stand and walk without experiencing any fatigue, tension or pain. But perfect posture is a rare thing indeed!

Poor posture stems from a failure to counteract gravity effectively. It can manifest itself in various parts of the body. The head may be thrust forward; the shoulders may be rounded or hunched; the pelvis may be tilted backward or forward; the feet may be taking the weight of the body on the inner edge — the stance we call 'pigeon-toed'.

No two people will have identical postures and postural problems. Nevertheless, two broad types of common postural problems can be identified.

Sway back

This type of posture is more common in women. The pelvis tilts back and the head pushes forward. Frequently the abdomen sticks out as well. People with a sway back often have tightness in the front of the hips and the calves.

Slumping

In this type of posture the pelvis tilts under and the head protrudes forward. The shoulders are rounded, throwing the muscles of the upper back and chest out of alignment. People who slump often have tightness between the shoulderblades and in the hamstrings.

Perfect posture

In perfect posture the natural curves of the spine are in alignment. This places the least stress on ligaments, muscles and discs. When standing upright, think of keeping your ears over your shoulders, your shoulders over your hips, your hips over your knees and your knees over your heels. Your head floats up like a balloon above your body, gently lengthening your spine. Posture is dynamic, however, and the principles of perfect posture have to be applied to a full range of movements from sitting and walking to exercising.

> Keep your head level. Don't force it back or let it poke forwards.
> Watch out for carrying tension in your neck and shoulders. Think of softly drawing your shoulderblades down into a V shape against your ribcage.
> Let your arms fall loosely from your shoulders.
> Keep your abdomen lifted by tightening the transversus abdominis.
> Relax your knees. Keep your weight distributed evenly over your feet.

Pilates and posture

Inefficient posture leads to poor muscle tone in the lower back, which eventually gives way to weakness and pain in later life. This process is exacerbated by our sedentary habits. Fortunately, every kind of misalignment can be improved, no matter how rigid or weak you think you are. Pilates can help in several ways. Regular Pilates practice will help you to become more aware of how you hold your body whether you are standing, sitting or moving. The slow, controlled movements lubricate the spine and improve mobility. The stretching eases the tension in stiff muscles and promotes flexibility. Finally, the emphasis on developing core stability leads to good muscle tone in the lower back for a pain-free back for life.

THE NEUTRAL SPINE

THE neutral spine is the natural curve of the spine at the lumbar region — the small of the back — when you are standing upright.

Again, no two people are identical, so the neutral spine position varies from person to person. In Pilates you need to find your own neutral spine position, and then challenge it with a range of movements. The aim is to maintain your lumbar spine in the neutral position whatever the rest of your body is doing. If you slip out of neutral, you are probably using your global muscles instead of your core strength.

To find and become aware of your neutral spine position, start by lying on the floor, ideally on a nonslip yoga mat. Work gently and slowly to discover the lumbar curve that is right for you, the position in which you feel comfortable, strong and relaxed.

The next step is to discover your neutral spine position while you are standing upright. Again, take it slowly and be sure that you have really found the stance in which you are relaxed, strong and confident.

Your aim is to maintain your natural lumbar curve by contracting your front and back muscles equally. Take plenty of time, and really concentrate on how it feels when you have found your neutral spine.

After these preliminary steps you will be ready to start working on the exercise ball.

The human spine

The spine is a complex structure of small, round, hollow bones called the vertebrae. Through the hollow middle runs the spinal cord, which contains the nerve connections that carry messages from the brain to all parts of the body. The vertebrae are cushioned from each other by discs of elastic tissue, forming a strong yet flexible column that enables us to bend, stretch and lift.

The normal spine has several natural curves:

> **THE CERVICAL CURVE**
  — the inward curve at the neck;

> **THE THORACIC CURVE**
  — the outward curve at the upper back;

> **THE LUMBAR CURVE**
  — the inward curve at the small of the back;

> **THE SACRAL CURVE**
  — the inward curve at the base of the spine.
  (This curve is formed by a comparatively rigid bone called the sacrum; some anatomists do not regard it as a spinal curve.)

Finding neutral in the supine position

Lie on your back with your knees bent and your knees and heels aligned with your hip sockets.

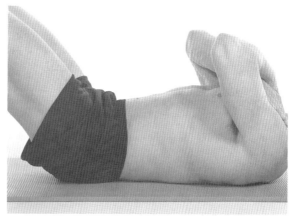

Gently flatten the small of your back to the floor.

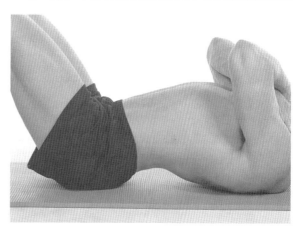

Arch the small of your back up from the floor.

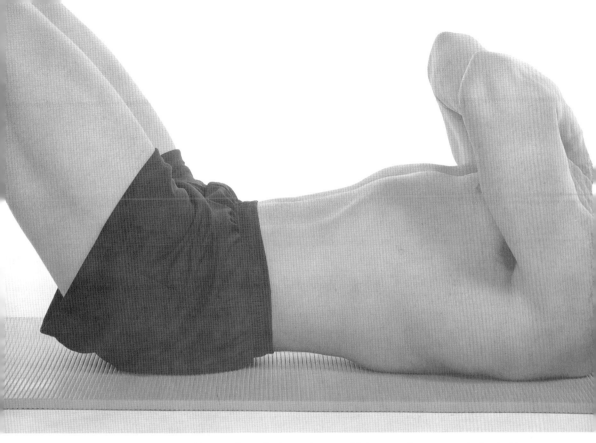

Alternate between the two positions until you find the halfway point. This should be close to your neutral spine position or the natural curve of your lumbar spine when you are standing correctly.

For some people the space between the small of the back and the floor will be scarcely perceptible. For others, it will be wide enough to push a hand through.

In some Pilates exercises you are instructed to imprint the spine. This action involves drawing the pelvis and ribcage towards each other, shortening the rectus abdominis and the obliques and pressing the spine into the mat. The transversus abdominis remains engaged throughout. As the action of imprinting the spine recruits a greater amount of abdominal muscle, it provides greater stability for more challenging work.

Finding neutral in the upright position

Stand upright and focus your attention on your pelvis, imagining that it is a bucket full of water.

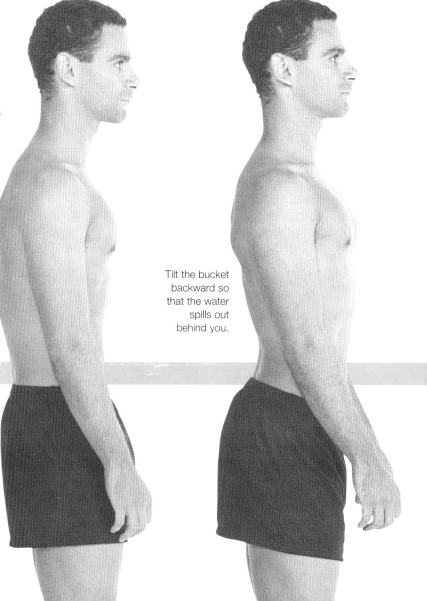

Tilt the bucket forward so that the water spills out in front of you.

Tilt the bucket backward so that the water spills out behind you.

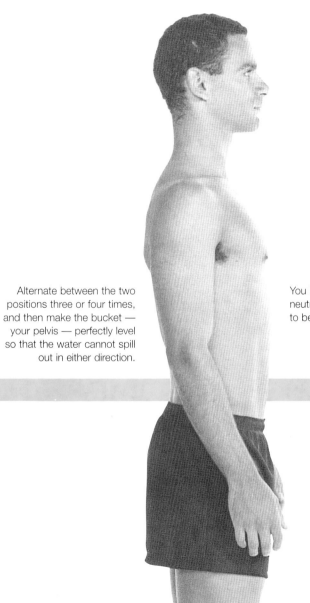

Alternate between the two positions three or four times, and then make the bucket — your pelvis — perfectly level so that the water cannot spill out in either direction.

You have now found your neutral spine, and are ready to begin working on the ball.

COMBINING Pilates techniques with work on the exercise ball is one of the most effective ways of building functional strength and core stability. By introducing an element of instability, working on the ball challenges your body to coordinate your various muscle groups, especially those of your core.

What is functional strength?

Functional strength is the strength that we draw on in our everyday life. At home or in the workplace, driving in the rush hour or setting off on holidays, struggling through a crowded supermarket or strolling along the beach — every single activity makes demands on your body, and your level of functional strength determines how efficiently you cope and how much you achieve.

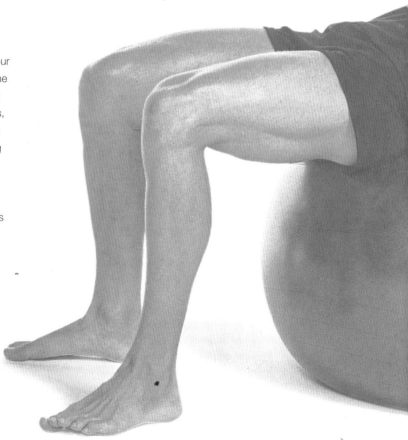

Think of pushing weights on a bench press. Your back is braced and stabilised against the bench so that you can focus on the global muscles of your chest and abdomen. Without that back support you will have to reduce the weight load by about two thirds. That is the measure of your functional strength.

Coordination and motor skills are important too. Combining Pilates with ball work develops these as well. Pilates movements challenge motor skills and the ball provides an unstable surface that challenges body balance and improves your coordination. Pilates and the ball operate together in a powerful harmony to promote functional fitness.

THE EXERCISE BALL

THE exercise ball, also known as the Swiss ball, the fitball, the mediball or the stability ball, has been around since the 1930s.

Invented in Italy by toymaker Aquilino Cosani, the ball is now enjoying ever-increasing popularity as an adjunct for training. In recent years it has become standard equipment, not only for functional fitness training but for physiotherapy and rehabilitation after sports injuries. Ball work is now as mainstream as weight-training. There are even desk workers who choose to replace their ergonomic chairs with a ball.

Training with the ball activates the core stabilising muscles more quickly and effectively than any other training method. This is because the ball provides an unstable base of support. The deep muscles around the spine have to work hard to maintain alignment and keep the ball steady, and this activity leads to greater core strength and stability.

Many athletes incorporate core training on the ball into their daily routine. Golfing superstar Tiger Woods takes one with him wherever he goes.

Buying your ball

There are many balls on the market, but the most important considerations when choosing one are the quality of the materials and the size that you select.

Don't stint on quality. A cheap ball may be too fragile and slippery for safety. Your ball should be made of durable, burst-resistant plastic with firm, strongly welded seams and a tight-fitting, well designed plug. You will also need a manual air pump or an air compressor to inflate your ball. Another useful piece of equipment is a nonslip yoga mat.

Balls are available in various sizes, and it is important both to select one that is the right size for your height and weight, and to inflate to the correct height for you. A ball that is the wrong height may lead to poor body alignment and potential injury.

When you are seated correctly on your ball, your thighs should be angled slightly downward from the hip to the knee. This frees the pelvic area, whereas sitting at a right angle would block the pelvis and inhibit movement.

Inflating your ball

Inflate your ball at room temperature. The maximum pressure for the average ball is about 300 kg, which should feel very firm. It is much harder to work on a soft ball, as it does not provide enough support. Balls tend to deflate over time, so always check the pressure before you start your workout.

> Inflate your ball slowly, especially if you are using an air compressor.
> Inflate your ball to the height and diameter prescribed by the manufacturer.
> Always make sure that the sealing plug is firmly seated.
> To deflate your ball, exert a steady pull the on the sealing plug while moving it back and forth. (Some manufacturers supply a patented plug remover.)

What size to buy

Balls come in several sizes.
As a rough guide when you are buying a ball:
> if you are up to 175 cm tall, you will need a 55 cm ball;
> if you are over 175 cm tall, you will need a 65 cm ball.

29

Caring for your ball

Having invested in a ball, and possibly an air pump or compressor and a yoga mat, it is only commonsense to take good care of it.

- Keep your ball well away from sources of heat, such as radiators, lamps and direct sunshine.
- Do not let your ball come into contact with sharp edges, such as chair and table legs. Scratches and dents will weaken your ball and shorten its life.
- Clean your ball regularly with a mild detergent and a clean, soft cloth.

Your ball as a work chair

More and more people are finding that a ball makes an excellent substitute for an office chair when they are sitting and working, and you may decide that you would like to do this.

A word of warning, however: because almost all of us have to sit all day, we tend to slump with the head tilted forward, the shoulders rounded and hunched, and the lumbar curve pushed outward from the neutral spine position. Merely sitting on a ball to work will not automatically correct this, and if you do decide to use one instead of a chair you will find yourself starting to slouch after a few minutes, just as you would on a chair.

To work up to using your ball as a chair, start with 10 minutes on the ball and 10 minutes off, building up the time as you gradually feel more comfortable.

Benefits of the ball

> It can be adapted for all ages and fitness levels.

> It builds up strength, balance and mobility.

> It encourages correct posture and builds up core muscle strength by challenging the body to maintain perfect balance.

> It enhances body awareness.

> It enforces concentration to maintain balance, exercising the mind as well as the body.

> It promotes functional fitness.

> It stimulates the neuromuscular system.

> It helps to prevent injury by encouraging a full range of movement, and by strengthening the body from the core muscles to the global muscles that come into play when extra strength is required to reach or lift.

> It is suitable for individual or group work.

And it's fun!

FINDING NEUTRAL ON THE BALL

Sit slightly forward of the central point of the ball. This will allow the front of your pelvic floor to move freely, enabling you to find your neutral spine. Keep your shoulders and chest relaxed and soft. Place your feet shoulder-width apart, as a wide support base makes it easier to maintain the neutral spine position. Make sure that you do not stabilise the ball by wedging it with your feet.

Tilt your pelvis forwards and backwards, as in finding neutral in the supine or upright positions. Alternate between the two until you find your halfway point. Activate your centre and feel your head float up above a long spine.

Prone

Lie face down over the ball, supporting yourself with your hands and feet and bracing yourself with your elbows and knees. Keep your hands and feet spaced well apart to make it easier to maintain the neutral spine position.

Supine

Lie on your back on a firm, flat surface — on the mat, if you have one — with your feet on the ball and your legs straight, or with your calves or heels on the ball and your knees bent.

Sideways lying

Lie on your side, with the ball between your lower ribs
and your hips so that it supports your waist. Use your
feet and arms to stabilise yourself.

Work and play

The Pilates exercise program and the ball have been around for many years, but combining these two techniques to help you to develop functional fitness represents an entirely new way of equipping both your body and your mind to function with maximum efficiency.

In its original form, the Pilates program was an extremely demanding form of exercise that few but the exceptionally fit could undertake without risk of injury. But since those early days in New York, fitness trainers have adapted Pilates' method to suit all levels of fitness.

The ball, by contrast, began life as a toy for children, but has now become a valuable tool in helping people to build a strong, stable centre.

In combination, Pilates exercises and the challenge of working on the ball will allow you to develop a lean, supple, toned body, dynamic stability and a clear focus.

Enjoy the experience!

GETTING STARTED

YOU can easily devise a Pilates ball exercise program that is custom-designed for you, and that takes into account your fitness aims, your general health, your current fitness level and the amount of time and space you have available. Follow the general guidelines below to ensure that you are exercising safely and with maximum effectiveness.

Plan your Pilates ball program to last 40–45 minutes.

Set aside about an hour each day, preferably at around the same time of day, at a time when you can be fairly sure you won't be interrupted. Remember that all exercises require total concentration, and should be performed at a consistent speed throughout.

Choose a sequence of movements suitable for your fitness level.

Incorporate a variety of positions into your program to ensure that the various muscle groups get a balanced workout.

Begin your program with its easiest movements, and progress to a level that challenges you but does not make you struggle. Don't move on to the next exercise until you are satisfied with your performance of the current exercise.

REMEMBER: stop at once if you feel faint or dizzy, if you are in pain, or if you are short of breath.

Some do's and dont's

> **DO** have your general health and fitness checked if you have not exercised for a long time.

> **DO** start each workout with a warm-up, and finish with at least 10 minutes of stretching and relaxation.

> **DO** exercise only on a safe, level surface; a nonslip yoga mat is an ideal accessory for ball work.

> **DO** exercise with bare feet, or wearing shoes with nonslip soles; socks may cause slipping.

> **DO** give yourself enough space to work without having to stop and move things. You are exercising your mind as well as your body, and even minor distractions can be frustrating and counterproductive.

> **DON'T** use your ball near stairs or ramps.

> **DON'T** let your ball come in contact with sharp objects.

> **DON'T** carry on if you feel faint or dizzy, or if you are in pain or short of breath.

PLANNING A PROGRAM

YOU can combine the various exercises in COREPILATES in any number of ways. Before you start a Pilates session, plan ahead and identify the exercises you wish to complete. When you first start, choose exercises from the Warming up, On the mat and Stretching sections. As your technique improves, add exercises from the Building strength and Putting it all together sections. You do not need to be in a hurry to move on if you are a beginner. The essence of Pilates is a controlled focus on precise, smooth movements. This takes time to develop, but is well worth the effort.

Warming up

This is where you begin to draw your attention inward and take note of your breathing. The objective of these exercises is not only to prepare your muscles for activity by increasing circulation and loosening the joints, but also to settle your mind. Spend at least 10 minutes on your warm-up and perform at least four of the exercises. Make sure you include movements for the upper and lower body.

On the mat

This is the main part of the program. Aim to spend at least 20 minutes on the mat and perform at least five exercises, working both the upper and lower body. In general follow the order in which they appear in this section. Always begin with the Level 1 option, even if you are a seasoned Pilates practitioner, and do not progress until you are certain you have established good control.

Building strength

This section features more intense exercises that challenge your ability to move smoothly, particularly with the unstable environment provided by the ball. They are designed to increase the strength and endurance of your muscles. Choose at least two exercises and aim to spend 10 minutes or more working on them.

Putting it all together

The goal of this section is to introduce variety and to raise the intensity of your workout with longer movement cycles. As each exercises includes combinations of movements, do not attempt any of them until you are confident that you can perform each component with precision and control. Remember also that your body may be fatigued by the time you reach this section. Perform each exercise as a continuous, flowing movement, linking the components as smoothly as you can. Make sure there is plenty of room around you in order to move freely. Choose at least one exercise. As you grow more familiar with Pilates, you may wish to choreograph your own progressions to suit your training objectives. There is no maximum number of movements you can include, so enjoy the creative challenge.

Stretching

Stretching is a vital part of your Pilates workout. It releases tension and promotes flexibility and a full range of movement in your muscles. Perform all the exercises in this section and spend at least 10 minutes on them. Stretch once on each side, and repeat the stretch if you want to.

WARMING UP

> Sit tall on the ball in the neutral spine position. Your feet are hip-width apart. Lengthen your spine. Your arms are by your side.

> Stretch your right arm up and away from your body, breathing in and out once as you complete the circle. Move only the upper part of your body.

> Perform the same sequence with your left arm.

> Repeat 5 to 10 times on each side.

Focus

Keep the ball as still as you can. To check that you are moving only your upper body, place one arm on your ribcage as you circle the other arm.

> Sit on the ball in the neutral spine position. Your feet are hip-width apart. Lengthen your spine. Your arms are by your side.

> Perform circles with both arms simultaneously. Remember to move only the upper part of your body.

> Repeat 5 to 10 times.

Focus
Concentrate on your breathing, making sure that you take a breath in and take a breath out with each circle.

> Sit on the ball in the neutral
  spine position. Your feet are
  hip-width apart and your arms
  are extended to the side.

> Press down on the ball
  with your body and feel
  your spine lengthening.

> Swing your hips to the right,
  as though you are drawing
  a circle on the floor.

> Repeat swinging your
  hips to the left, keeping your
  floor circles the same size.

> Repeat 10 times
  on each side.

Focus
Move slowly and gently,
focusing on finding your
centre and making it work
for you. Imagine that you have
a glass of water on your head.
Challenge yourself to move
as freely as you can without
spilling the water.

> Sit on the ball in the neutral spine position. Your feet are hip-width apart. Lengthen your spine. Make sure your feet are directly below your knees.

> Hold your arms out low to the side. Pull your shoulderblades down in a soft V.

> Keeping your spine long and tall, activate your centre from your pelvis and raise your right leg, breathing out as you do so.

> Lower your leg, breathing in. Repeat with your left leg.

> Repeat 5 to 10 times with each leg.

Focus

Concentrate on using your centre to support and balance the weight of each leg as you raise it.

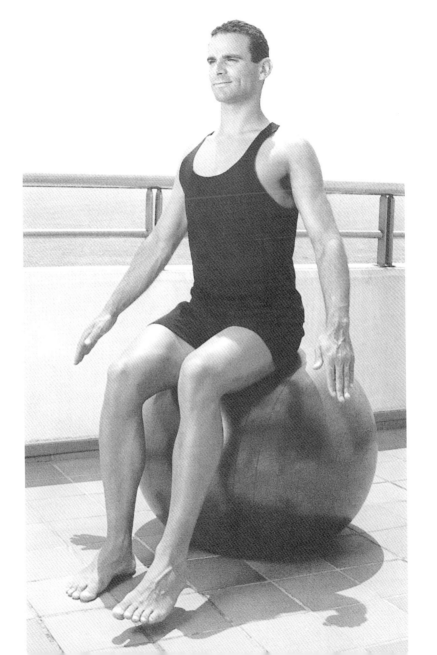

WALKING OUT TO BRIDGE

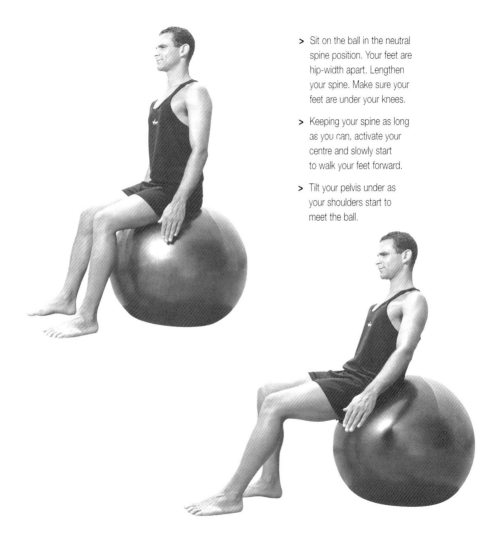

> Sit on the ball in the neutral spine position. Your feet are hip-width apart. Lengthen your spine. Make sure your feet are under your knees.

> Keeping your spine as long as you can, activate your centre and slowly start to walk your feet forward.

> Tilt your pelvis under as your shoulders start to meet the ball.

Focus

Support your back by strongly contracting your centre. The closer together your legs are, the harder it is to balance and the harder you must work the core muscles. Challenge yourself by performing the exercise keeping your legs as close together as possible without losing control of the movement.

> Form a bridge, with your head, neck, spine and pelvis horizontal and in-line.

> Return to the seated position keeping your torso long and tall without collapsing your body.

> Repeat 5 to 10 times.

> Start as for the leg lift.

> Raise one leg lift a step while simultaneously raising the opposite arm.

> Keep your shoulders relaxed and low, your core activated and your ribcage expanded.

> Breathe out as you lift your leg and your arm, and breathe in as you lower them.

> Repeat with your left leg and your right arm.

> Repeat 5 to 10 times on each side.

Focus
To challenge your body even further, try closing your eyes.

ON THE MAT

> Lie on the mat with knees
  bent and feet flat. Keep
  your neutral spine position
  and activate your centre.

> Keep your neck long and pull
  your shoulderblades down
  into a soft V.

> Hold the position for 10
  breaths, maintaining lateral
  thoracic breathing.

> From the same position, raise one leg so that your knee is above your hip and your shin parallel to the floor.

> Hold for 5 to 10 breaths. Lower your leg on an outward breath. Repeat with the other leg.

> Repeat 10 times on each leg.

Focus

This action is deceptively easy. The objective is to keep the spine still and to maintain a strong centre while lifting the leg. Do not allow your deep abdominal muscles to loosen while raising and lowering the leg, but focus on controlling your centre.

> Lie on the mat as for level 1.
  Activate your centre to begin.

> Raise one leg, then imprint
  your spine on the mat,
  breathe out and raise
  your other leg.

> Keep your legs level.

> Hold for 5 to 10 breaths, and then lower first one leg, then the other.

> If you start to shake, drop down to level 1 again.

Focus

Concentrate on keeping your core muscles strongly contracted throughout and maintaining lateral thoracic breathing. Imprinting your spine on the mat helps to strengthen your abdominal muscles and provides greater control over the action.

THE HUNDRED ON THE BALL
Level 1

> Lie on the mat with both calves resting on the ball. Keep your neutral spine position and activate your centre. Take 10 breaths, expanding your ribcage sideways.

> Float one leg off the ball, keeping your pelvis as still as you can. Hold the position for five breaths, then lower your leg. Repeat with the other leg.

> Repeat 10 times on each leg.

Focus
Keep your neck relaxed and your shoulderblades pulled down in a soft V. Keep your breathing slow and steady.

- Hold the ball between your legs and grip it firmly.
- Imprint your spine into the mat and lift the ball from the floor.
- Return to the neutral spine position and keep the ball raised for 5 to 10 breaths.
- Repeat 10 times.

Focus

This level strongly recruits your global muscles. If you sense that they are doing all the work, go back to level 1.

> Lie on your side on the mat with your lower arm extended and your upper arm curled gently over your body to the floor.

> Hold the ball between your ankles, stretching your legs away from you and keeping your waist slightly raised from the mat.

> Make sure you are in the neutral spine position. Keep your hips and shoulders in line.

> Activate your centre and breathe out as you lift the ball from the mat. Then breathe in as you lower the ball back to the mat.

> Repeat 5 to 10 times on each side.

Focus

Stay in alignment and don't allow your legs to swing backwards or fowards. Avoid tension in your neck and shoulders. When you are stable, challenge yourself further by placing your upper arm along your upper side.

> Lie on the mat with both feet on the floor in the neutral spine position.

> Raise one leg onto the ball so that your knee is above your hip. Activate your centre.

> Keeping the ball still, rotate your raised knee in a circle, breathing out on the outward movement and in on the inward movement.

> Repeat 10 times on each side.

Focus
Keep your neck long and relaxed and your shoulderblades pulled down in a soft V.

> Lie on the mat as for level 1, with both legs on the ball.

> Slowly float one leg off the ball, keeping your knee above your hip.

> Keep the raised leg still and rotate the leg that is on the ball.

> Repeat 10 times on each side.

Focus
Think of your knee as drawing the circle and allow the ball to lead the movement.

69

SHOULDER BRIDGE
Level 1

> Lie on the mat in the neutral spine position. Rest both calves on the ball and your arms on the floor, palms downward. Check that your shoulderblades are pulled down in a soft V.

> Breathe out and imprint your spine on the mat. Peel your back off the mat and lift your hips towards the ceiling, keeping the ball still.

> Breathe in, and then breathe out as you roll back down the mat and return your spine to the neutral position.

> Repeat 5 to 10 times.

> Add an extra challenge by stretching your arms out behind your head, palms upward.

Focus

Keep your hips level as you lift up. Concentrate on contracting your centre to maintain stability. Try not to contract your glutes, but use your core muscles to raise and lower your hips.

> Lie on the mat as for level 1, with both feet on the ball. Activate your centre to begin.

> Breathe out and Imprint your spine into the mat. Raise your hips as high as you can, keeping the ball still with your feet.

> Breathe in, and then breathe out as you lower yourself back onto the mat. Keep the ball as steady as you can.

> Repeat 5 to 10 times.

> Stretch your arms behind
  your head to raise the level
  of difficulty.

Focus
Performing the shoulder bridge with your feet on the
ball is more challenging than performing it with your
calves, as the area in contact with the ball is smaller.
Activate your core to keep your hips steady as you
raise and lower them.

REVERSE SHOULDER BRIDGE

> Walk out to a bridge position (pages 54-55).

> Activate your centre and breathe in. Breathe out as you roll your spine down the ball, following the shape of the ball with your back.

> Breathe in at the bottom, and then breathe out as you lift your hips back to the bridge position. Keep your hips level as you lift them up.

> Repeat 5 to 10 times.

Focus

Focus on keeping your spine elongated and your ribcage expanded. You should feel as though your back is moulding itself to the ball.

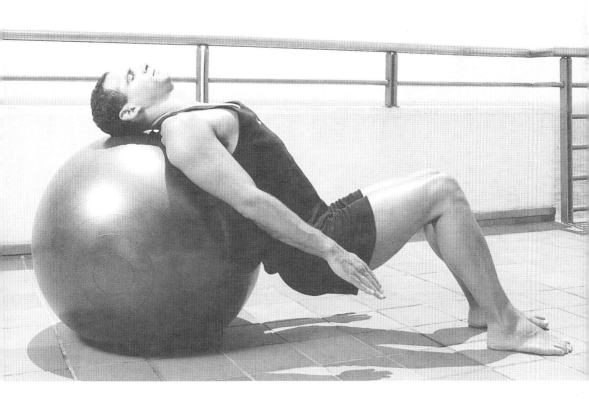

> Kneel with the ball at your left side and rest your body over it. Keep your hips and shoulders stacked on top of each other as you extend your right leg to the side in a parallel position. Stretch your right arm overhead.

> Activate your centre and breathe out as you lift your right leg to hip height. Point your toes.

> Draw a circle with your pointed toe, reaching your leg away from you. Breathe in and out to make one complete circle.

> Repeat 5 to 10 times.

> Flex your foot and reverse direction, using your heel to draw the circle.

> Repeat 5 to 10 times.

> Repeat on the left leg, resting the right side of your body over the ball.

Focus

Keep your shoulderblades pulled down in a soft V. Pay particular care to the shoulder of the arm that is stretched overhead. Lengthen your body out of your hips. Make sure that the leg that is circling goes all the way behind you as well as in front.

> Sit tall and straight with your
knees bent and your feet on
the floor, holding the ball
between your knees and
ankles. Squeeze the ball
lightly and grasp the backs of
your thighs with your hands.

> Breathe in as you tilt your pelvis under and roll back towards the mat. Breathe out as you return to the seated position.

> Repeat 5 to 10 times.

> Increase the level of difficulty by holding the ball in front of you as you roll back.

Focus

This is a good exercise if you have a tight lower back. Roll back only as far as your spine will allow, especially when holding the ball in front of you. If you need more air, breathe in at the top of the movement, breathe out as you roll back, breathe in at the bottom of the movement, and breathe out as you return to the seated position.

> Lie on the mat, holding the ball between your arms. Lengthen your legs and take the ball back behind your head as far as you can while maintaining the neutral spine position. Pull your shoulders down into a soft V.

> Activate your centre and breathe in as you raise the ball towards the ceiling.

> Breathe out and imprint your spine into the mat as you lower the ball to the top of your legs.

> Slowly roll your body upward, peeling your spine away from the mat.

> Bend smoothly forward, pushing down lightly on the ball as it rolls along your legs. Breathe in, and then breathe out as you reverse the movement and return to the neutral spine position.

> Repeat 5 to 10 times.

Focus
Aim for a smooth, controlled movement, with your neck and shoulders relaxed.

on the mat

> Sit tall and long on the floor
  with your legs extended. Hold
  the ball out in front of you.

> Breathe in and activate your centre. Breathe out as you twist your torso and the ball sideways, following the centre of the ball with your eyes. Breathe in as you return to the centre, and then breathe out to twist in the opposite direction.

> Try to make your movement a bit bigger with each twist, as if you were a balloon expanding.

> Repeat 5 to 10 times on each side.

Focus
If your lower back is very tight, you can perform this exercise with your knees bent and your feet flat on the floor.

ROLLING LIKE A BALL

> Sit on the mat with the ball held between your slightly raised knees. Put your arms around the ball and round your body to the shape of the ball.

> Holding onto the ball, start to roll back, keeping your body in its rounded shape.

> Roll right back, and then return to the seated position.

> Repeat 5 to 10 times.

Focus

Perform this exercise as smoothly and evenly as you can, breathing in as you roll back and out as you return to the seated position.

> Lie on the mat with your
  knees bent and your spine
  in the neutral position.
  Activate your centre.
  Place one foot on the ball.

> As you breathe out, stretch
  out the leg that is on the ball.
  Focus on pushing your leg in
  a straight line and keeping
  your spine long.

> Breathe in as you pull
  your leg back.

> Repeat 10 times
  on each side.

Focus

Keep your spine in neutral
and maintain a strong centre.

> Lie on the mat as for level 1
> with both feet on the ball.
> Activate your centre to begin.

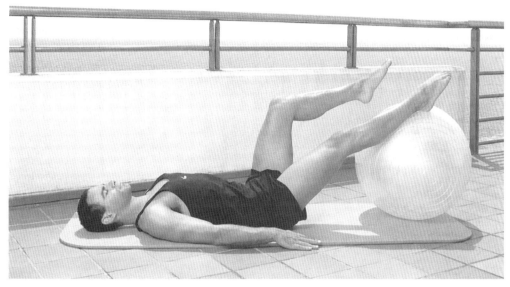

> Stretch one leg out and use it to hold the ball steady as you reach the other leg away from you.

> Breathe out as you reach away and in as you pull back.

> Repeat 10 times on each side.

Focus

As you develop better abdominal control, test how low you can take the raised leg without losing the neutral spine position.

> Lie on the mat with your knees slightly bent and your spine in the neutral position. Place both feet on the ball. Activate your centre.

> Raise your arms slightly, with palms down.

> As you breathe out, stretch both legs away from you.

> Breathe in as you pull the legs back.

> Repeat 10 times.

Focus
Keep your shoulderblades pulled down in a soft V.

> Lie on the mat as for level 1.

> Circle your arms back while you stretch your legs away.

> Keep your neutral spine position and breathe out and in once for each stretch.

> Repeat 10 times.

Focus

Make sure that your arms and legs work together.

> Lie on the mat with your
  knees bent and your spine
  in the neutral position.
  Activate your centre. Pull
  your shoulderblades down
  in a soft V. Place both feet
  on the ball.

> Keeping the ball still, raise and lower each leg in turn to just touch the ball.

> Breathe in as you raise one leg and out as you lower the other.

> Repeat 5 to 10 times on each side.

Focus
Keep the raised leg at a right angle.

> Sit on the ball in the neutral
  spine position. Your feet are
  hip-width apart. Lengthen
  your spine. Place one arm on
  top of the other in front of
  you, cossack-style.

> Slowly twist to one side while
  you breathe out. Breathe in
  and then increase the rotation
  while you breathe out.

> Return slowly to the centre while you breathe in. Be conscious of your spine lengthening.

> Repeat 10 times to each side.

> Increase the level of difficulty by extending your arms to the side. Keep your shoulderblades pulled down in a soft V.

Focus
Keep your neck long. Don't let your hips twist with you.

BUILDING STRENGTH

> Stand in the neutral spine
position holding the ball out in
front of you with your arms
extended and slightly raised.
Bend foward, lowering the ball
until it touches the ground.

> Bend your knees until you are kneeling on the mat, with your hands on the ball in front of you.

> As you breathe out, lower your body into a box position. Flex your elbows outward and push against the ball, keeping it as still as you can.

> Reverse smoothly back to the standing position.

> Repeat 5 to 10 times.

Focus
Activate your centre to maintain alignment throughout this sequence.

> Start as for level 1.

> Roll down to the box position. Slide forward over the ball and place your hands on the mat in front of it.

> Raise your legs into a plank position. Activate your centre.

> Push up in this position maintaining a strong centre.

> Reverse smoothly back to the standing position.

Focus

Make sure your body is in a straight line from head to toe in the plank position. The further forward over the ball you roll, the harder the push-up. Work towards having your insteps on the ball.

> Kneel on the mat, leaning slightly forward with your hands resting on the ball.

> Push the ball away from you, keeping your shoulderblades pulled down in a soft V and your spine in the neutral position.

> Activate your centre to maintain alignment. Hold the position for 30 to 90 seconds.

> Return to the kneeling position.

> Repeat 5 to 10 times.

Focus
Keep your neck and shoulders relaxed and your breathing deep and even.

> Start as for level 1

> Support your forearms on the ball while you raise your body onto your toes, keeping your legs and body in a straight line.

> Raise first one foot and then the other, keeping the ball steady.

> Reverse smoothly to the kneeling position.

> Repeat 5 to 10 times.

Focus

Maintain a strong centre while you raise your legs. Hold the ball as still as you can.

> Kneel on the mat with the ball in front of you.

> Roll forward over the ball into a plank position. Make sure your body forms a straight line from head to toe. Your arms are straight and your wrists are in line with your shoulders. Activate your centre to protect your lower back.

> Hinge at the hip joint and lift into a pike position. Lift your hips as high as you can.

> Slowly return to the plank position.

> Repeat 5 to 10 times.

Focus
Use your abdominal muscles to roll the ball in to the pike position.

> Lie prone over the ball with your arms and legs straight. Maintain equal weight on all four. Your feet are hip-width apart. Keep your spine long and your shoulders pulled down in a soft V. Activate your centre.

> Breathe out as you lift your right arm off the floor. Breathe in as you lower it again. Keep the ball as still as you can as you change to the other side.

> Repeat 5 to 10 times on each side.

> Another variation of this exercise is to keep your arms on the floor and lift your legs.

> Breathe out as you lift the right leg and breathe in as you lower it again. Keep the ball as still as you can as you change to the other side.

> Repeat 5 to 10 times on each side.

Focus

Pay attention to your centre throughout to maintain a neutral spine. Think of lifting your abs away from the ball.

> Start as for level 1.

> Breathe out as you lift the
  right arm and the left leg.
  Breathe in as you lower
  them again.

> Repeat 5 to 10 times
  on each side.

Focus

Slide your shoulder down your
back as you raise your arm.
Feel your muscles in your arms
and legs lengthen before you
start to lift them. Height is not
as important as length.

> Start as for level 2.

> Breathe out as you raise both arms at the same time, keeping your feet on the ground at hip-width apart. Breathe in as you lower them again.

> Another variation is to keep your arms on the floor and lift your legs.

> Breathe out as you raise both legs, keeping your hands on the floor. Breathe in as you lower them again.

Focus

Keep the movement as continuous as you can in both variations. If you start to take too much strain in your shoulders or cannot maintain the contraction in your centre, return to levels 1 or 2.

> Kneel next to the ball. Keep the ball close to your thighs and bend your body over it, maintaining a right angle. Place your arms next to your side, palms up.

> Activate your centre and lengthen your spine. Breathe out as you lift into a back extension. Breathe in as you lower over the ball.

> Repeat 5 to 10 times.

Focus

Keep your neck long and your shoulders pulled down in a soft V. Protect your lower back by maintaining the contraction in your centre. Let your breath dictate the speed of the movement.

> Start as for level 1.

> Place your hands behind your head to add extra weight to the movement. Stretch your legs out with your feet hip-width apart.

> Activate your centre. Breathe out as you lift into the back extension and breathe in as you lower over the ball.

> Repeat 5 to 10 times.

Focus

Check that your shoulderblades stay down your spine.
Keep a long distance between your ears and shoulders.
Keep the movement as continuous as you can.

> Kneel with the ball at your left side. Bend sideways over the ball and extend your right leg to the side in a parallel position. Cross your arms over your chest.

> Activate your centre. Breathe out as you lift your body. Breathe in as you lower back over the ball.

> Repeat 5 to 10 times on each side.

Focus
Keep your spine long as you lift up. Pay attention to your centre to maintain a neutral spine.

> Start as for level 1.

> Place your hands behind your head to add extra weight to the movement.

> Breathe out as you lift your body and breathe in as you lower back over the ball.

> Repeat 5 to 10 times on each side.

Focus
Keep your shoulders pulled down your spine in a soft V and your elbows opened.

> Start as for level 2.

> Stretch your arms
  above your head.

> Breathe out as you lift your
  body and breathe in as you
  lower back over the ball.

> Repeat 5 to 10 times
  on each side.

Focus

Slide your shoulderblades down your spine as you raise
your arms. Check you are not taking any strain in your
shoulders. Lift out of your hips and keep your spine long.

PUTTING IT ALL TOGETHER

> Lie on your back on the
  mat in a neutral spine
  position, holding the
  ball in front of you (1).

> Breathe in and raise
  the ball overhead (2).

> Breathe out and bring
  the ball forward towards
  your legs. Roll up through
  the spine, sliding the ball
  over your legs (3).

> Breathe in and stretch
  forward over your legs (4).

> Breathe out and uncurl
  your spine into a seated
  position, holding the ball
  in front of you (5).

> Breathe in and twist the
  ball around to one side,
  keeping the ball in the
  centre of your body. Lift
  out of your hips and pull
  your shoulderblades down
  into a soft V (6).

> Breathe out and return
  to centre. Repeat to the
  other side.

> Bend your legs and pull
  the ball close against
  your body (7).

> Breathe in as you roll
  back with the ball (8).

> Breathe out as you roll
  up again (9).

> Breathe in and stretch your
  legs out in front of you,
  lifting out of the hips (10).
  Breathe out and roll back
  down to the starting position.

> Repeat 5 to 10 times.

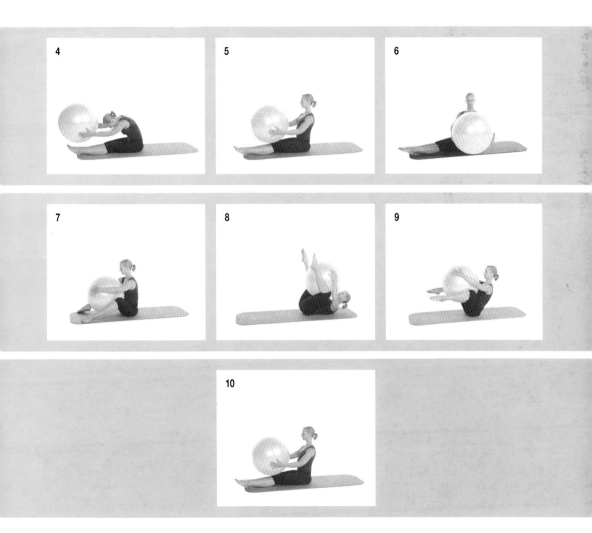

PUSH-UP –
LEG PULL PRONE – PIKE

1

2

3

> Stand tall in a neutral spine position, holding the ball out in front of you with your arms extended and slightly raised (1).

> Breathe in and slowly roll down through your spine towards the floor. Imagine that there is a wall behind you from which you are peeling away one vertebra at a time. Try to keep your legs straight (2).

> As the ball touches the ground, bend your knees and put your hands on top of it. Slide forward and put your hands on the mat in front of it (3).

> Breathe out and walk your body out into a plank position (4).

> Activate your centre and check that your shoulderblades are flat against your ribs and your hips are level (5).

> Breathe in as you lower your body and breathe out as you push up (6).

> Breathe in and lengthen your muscles. Breathe out and raise one leg (7).

> Breathe in and lower the leg. Breathe out and raise the other leg. Keep the ball as steady as you can and hold your centre strongly.

> Breathe in and return the foot to the ball. Breathe out and hinge at the hip joint, lifting your hips as high as you can into a pike position (8).

> Breathe in and return to the plank position (9).

> Breathe out and walk your hands back until you are standing again. Breathe in and slowly uncurl your spine to the starting position (10).

> Repeat 5 to 10 times.

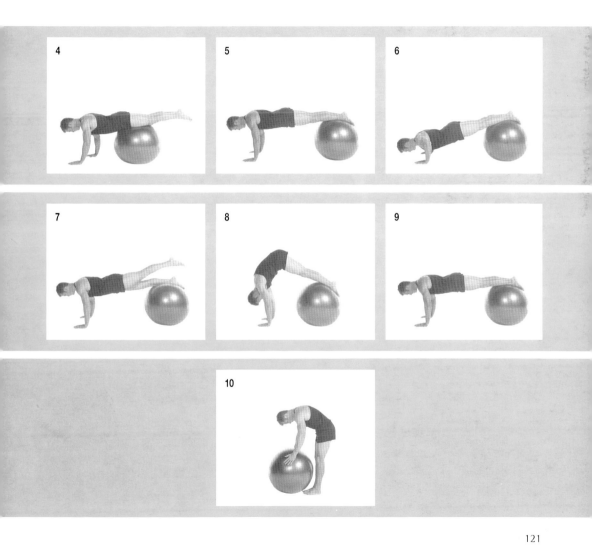

> Start prone over the ball with your legs straight and your arms down by your side (1).

> Breathe in and lengthen your muscles and activate your centre.

> Breathe out and lift into a back extension (2).

> Hold your centre strongly, breathe in and bring the ball around to the left side, turning your body. Bend your left knee and extend your right leg to the side in a parallel position (3).

> Breathe out and raise the leg to hip height (4).

> Breathe in and lengthen your muscles and check your centre. Breathe out and bring the leg forward in front of your hip. Keep the ball as still as you can (5).

> Breathe in and take the leg back to the side. Breathe out and lower the foot to the mat.

> Breathe in and come to your knees. Breathe out and carry the ball over your head to the other side, lifting out of your hips. Make sure you hold your centre strongly (6).

> Breathe in and tuck the ball under your right side. Extend your left leg to the side (7).

> Breathe out and raise the leg to hip height (8).

> Breathe in and lengthen your muscles and check your centre. Breathe out and bring the leg forward in front of your hip. Keep the ball as still as you can (9).

> Breathe in and take the leg back to the side. Breathe out and lower the foot to the mat.

> Breathe out and turn your body around to the starting position on the other side (10).

> Repeat 5 to 10 times.

> Sit on the ball in the neutral spine position. Your feet are hip-width apart. Lengthen your spine (1).

> Circle both arms back, keeping the ball as still as you can. Breathe out on the half circle and breathe in to complete the movement (2).

> Breathe out as you walk your feet forward slowly, keeping your arms lifted in front of you and your spine long (3).

> Tilt your pelvis under as your shoulders meet the ball in the bridge position. Check that your head, neck, spine and pelvis are horizontal and in-line (4).

> Circle both arms back in this position, keeping the ball as still as you can. Breathe out on the half circle and breathe in to bring the arms around in front of you (5).

> Breathe out and round your spine against the ball, dropping your pelvis towards the floor. Keep the ball as still as you can (6).

> Breathe in as you lift your hips back to the bridge position. Hold your centre strongly to maintain stability and protect your lower back (7).

> Breathe out as you return to the starting position.

> Repeat 5 to 10 times.

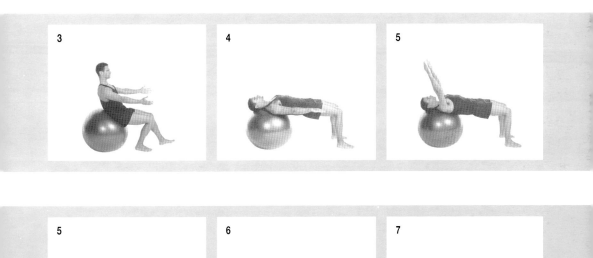

STRETCHING

> Sit on the mat in the neutral spine position with your legs crossed and your arms outstretched on the ball in front of you.

> Breathe out as you round your back to push the ball away. Then slowly straighten up to the sitting position.

> Repeat 5 to 10 times

Focus

Feel the stretch across your upper back. Breathe slowly and keep your neck long. Use the ball to gently increase the stretch.

> Start as for level 1 with your legs extended at each side of the ball.

> Breathe out as you round your back to push the ball away. Then slowly straighten up to the sitting position.

> Repeat 5 to 10 times

Focus

Try to keep your knees and pelvis as motionless as possible, the backs of your knees flat and your pelvis parallel to the floor, not tilted backwards. The more flexible you are, the further foward you will be able to stretch. Move slowly and don't force the stretch.

> Kneel on the mat with the ball on your left side. Make sure that your hands are under your shoulders and your knees are under your hips. Keep the neutral spine position and activate your centre.

> Place your left forearm on the ball, level with your shoulder.

> Breathe out and turn away from the ball until you feel a stretch in your chest.

> Hold the stretch for 30 seconds, taking deep, slow breaths.

> Repeat on the other side.

Focus

You can vary the position of the stretch by placing your hand on the ball and keeping the arm straight. Do not lock the elbow. Bend the underneath elbow to stretch the chest muscle.

> Sit tall on the ball in the neutral spine position. Your feet are hip-width apart.

> Extend the left leg out in front of you. Flex the foot and place your hands on the opposite knee.

> Keep your spine long and your shoulders pulled down in a soft V. Breathe out and stretch forward over your leg.

> Hold the stretch for 30 seconds, taking deep, slow breaths. Try to extend further forward with each exhalation.

> Repeat on the other side.

Focus
Activate your centre to prevent your spine from rounding over. The objective is to extend forward from the hips in a straight line.

> Place the ball behind you. Bend forward and take your hands to the floor with your knees bent. Extend your right leg behind you on the ball.

> Breathe in, activate your centre and push your hips down. Keep your spine long and your shoulderblades pulled down in a soft V.

> Breathe out, contract your glutes and push your foot on the ball.

> Hold the stretch for 30 seconds, taking deep, slow breaths.

> Repeat on the other side.

Focus
Relax your neck. Make sure your hips are square throughout.

> Place the ball behind you. Kneel down on your right leg and extend the left leg in front of you. Keep the knee directly over the ankle. Place your right foot on the ball behind you.

> Breathe in and bring your body upright. Lift up out of your hips. Place your hands on your left leg.

> Breathe out then in, activate your centre and pull your foot in towards your body.

> Hold the stretch for 30 seconds, taking deep slow breaths.

> Repeat on the other side.

Focus

Maintain a strong centre to avoid arching the spine. This is an advanced stretch. You may prefer to hold on to something to keep you steady until you have improved your stability.

> Sit on the ball and walk
> forward into a shoulder bridge
> position. Make sure your
> head, neck, spine and pelvis
> are in line and horizontal.

> Activate your centre.
> Breathe in and raise your
> arms above your shoulders.

> Breathe out and take
> your arms above your head.
> Pull your shoulders down
> in a soft V.

> Breathe in and straighten your legs, stretching your spine over the ball.

> Hold the stretch for 30 seconds, taking deep, slow breaths.

> Slowly roll back up to the starting position.

Focus
Open the chest and expand the ribcage as you breathe in to the stretch. Relax your face and neck.

Liz Dene is Education and Convention Program Manager for the Australian Fitness Network, and is actively involved in programming international events and developing training courses. She has a degree in Human Movement Studies from the Sydney University of Technology, and has expertise in all areas of training and fitness. Liz merges traditional fitness practices with a holistic approach to well being.

Shannan Ponton comes from a sporting background. Born in Sydney, he has worked as strength-connect for the North Sydney Rugby League team ('the Bears'), and has accompanied the team on international tours. He has been a master trainer for Les Mills Pump, and for the past twelve years has worked as a personal trainer and fitness instructor in Sydney's northern suburbs.

Zosha Piotrowski is a national and international presenter in group fitness and personal training. She runs her own instructor training academy and is a lecturer and presenter for the Australian Fitness Network; both are based in Sydney. Trained by Michael King, Zosha is also a Pilates Institute (UK) Master Trainer, delivering Pilates training throughout Australia.

Tony Boutazy is a Sydney-based fitness coach and an education and training consultant, lecturer and author for the Australian Fitness Network. He holds a Bachelor in Human Movement Studies from the Australian Catholic University and is a member of the National Strength and Conditioning Association and the American College of Sports Medicine. He specialises in advanced exercise programs for strength, endurance and weight loss.

Australian-born **Olivia Bell** graduated from the ballet school of the Paris Opéra in 1995 and then joined the Australian Ballet, where she danced the Lilac Fairy *(Aurora's Wedding)*, Lescaut's mistress *(Manon)*, Queen of the Wilis *(Giselle)* and The Prayer *(Coppélia)*. In 1996 she was awarded a Khitercs Foundation scholarship, enabling her to study abroad. In 2002 she was chosen to perform in the première of Robbins' *Other Dances*, and she also danced Act III of *Swan Lake* for The Dancers Company Tour.

Hugh Hamilton began his professional life as a *Vogue* photographer, but soon found that he cared more about women than their clothes. He now works in advertising, which he loves, but theatre and dance have been a profound influence on the way he works: drama and shadow, with the human body as his inspiration, inform his work.

Jon Reid is a photographer on contract to the *Sydney Morning Herald*. His other books for ABC Books are *Fix your back*, *Strong to the core* and *Reality food*.

ACKNOWLEDGMENTS

Many thanks to all my Australian colleagues and friends, especially Nigel and Lisa Champion whose company, Australian Fitness Network, had the faith to bring me to Australia. Thanks also to Liz Dene who has organised the training and courses with us for the last few years. It is because of them and their great team that I have been able to bring my work to Australia. I must also thank my wonderful team in London who make it possible to leave the Pilates Institute.

Of course, a book is the combined effort of many individuals. I would like to extend my gratitude to

> My commissioning editor at ABC Books, Jill Brown, and her talented team:
  designer Ingo Voss and editor Janet Healey

> My American friends Matthew Lore and Sue McCloskey at Marlowe & Company

> The photographers, Hugh Hamilton and Jon Reid

> The models, Olivia Bell, Tony Boutagy, Liz Dene, Zosha Piotrowski and Shannon Ponton

> Rozane Lazzari at Brazil Body for her generous use of the lovely clothes for the Pilates models
  (rozane@brazilbody.com)

> Bloch Dancewear Specialists for dressing Olivia Bell

> The Harbord Diggers Club for the balcony by the ocean

Michael King
www.pilates-institute.com